CONTENTS

1 CHRISTMAS
(Weihnachten)

Composed 1845

10

2 NEW YEAR

(Am Neujahrstage)

Composed 25 December 1843

Andante

SOPRANO 1

Lord God, thou art our sal - va - tion e - ver - more.
Herr, Gott, du bist uns - re Zu - flucht für und für.

SOPRANO 2

Lord God, thou art our sal - va - tion e - ver - more.
Herr, Gott, du bist uns - re Zu - flucht für und für.

ALTO 1

Lord God, thou art our sal - va - tion e - ver - more.
Herr, Gott, du bist uns - re Zu - flucht für und für.

ALTO 2

Lord God, thou art our sal - va - tion e - ver - more.
Herr, Gott, du bist uns - re Zu - flucht für und für.

TENOR 1

Lord God, thou art our sal - va - tion e - ver - more.
Herr, Gott, du bist uns - re Zu - flucht für und für.

TENOR 2

Lord God, thou art our sal - va - tion e - ver - more. E'en be - fore the
Herr, Gott, du bist uns - re Zu - flucht für und für. E - he denn die

BASS 1

Lord God, thou art our sal - va - tion e - ver - more.
Herr, Gott, du bist uns - re Zu - flucht für und für.

BASS 2

Lord God, thou art our sal - va - tion e - ver - more.
Herr, Gott, du bist uns - re Zu - flucht für und für.

Andante

Keyboard Reduction

14

16

3 ASCENSION DAY

(Am Himmelfahrtstage)

Composed 9 October 1846

4 PASSIONTIDE
(In der Passionszeit)

Composed 14 February 1844

30

5 ADVENT
(Im Advent)

Composed 5 October 1846

38

6 GOOD FRIDAY
(Am Charfreitage)

Composed 18 February 1844

42

Originated and printed by
Halstan & Co. Ltd., Amersham, Bucks., England

ISBN 0-19-395322-6

9 780193 953222

CHURCH MUSIC SOCIETY REPRINTS No. 58
Honorary General Editor: Richard Lyne

FELIX MENDELSSOHN
(1809-1847)

Six Seasonal Motets
Op. 79

for 8-part choir

Adapted to English words by
Richard Marlow

Published for the
CHURCH MUSIC SOCIETY
by
OXFORD UNIVERSITY PRESS
Great Clarendon Street, Oxford OX2 6DP

PREFACE

Mendelssohn composed these motets during the mid-1840s for the Cathedral Choir of Berlin. The text of each was chosen with a particular church season or holy day in mind, but most are also suitable for more general use.

They are meant to be sung unaccompanied. The editorial keyboard reduction printed below the vocal parts is intended only as a rehearsal aid, although it will serve as the basis for a suitable organ accompaniment if needed. In view of the thick texture, wide spacing, and frequent part-crossing, it is impossible to provide a two-stave reduction which reproduces throughout the original disposition of the eight voices in a way that is both clear to read and convenient to play. Where literal transcription is unsatisfactory, the keyboard score is accordingly thinned out, in general preserving essential harmony-notes and leads, as well as the outer-sounding parts, but conflating the inner voices.

The English translation now provided attempts to mirror as faithfully as possible the accentuation, rhythm, phrase-lengths, and musical focus of the original German. Mendelssohn's underlay and textual repetitions are adopted unaltered, except in No. 6, bar 8, where the word 'cross' replaces the two-syllable German 'kreuze'; and in No. 3, bars 11–13 (Tenor 2) and 18–19 (Tenor 1), where 'zu Ewigkeit', rendered elsewhere as 'world without end', repeats the phrase 'for evermore' ('von Ewigkeit') – this making better rhythmic sense in these particular contexts.

This edition is based on the text of these motets found in *F. Mendelssohn-Bartholdy: Werke*, Series 14 (Leipzig, 1874–7). The music was first published in 1848.

I should like to thank Watkins Shaw, Robert Atwell, Clare Wallace, and Mary Hitch for their help in preparing this publication.

October 1982

Richard Marlow
Cambridge